MW00861292

IMPORTANT

If you have a print copy of this book, or someone emailed you a digital version, it's very important to follow the link below to get on the mailing list to get the free bonus material and follow up material that comes with this book! You don't want to miss it! You will receive more great recipes, any and all updates to the book, as well as tons of great healthy living tips.

https://DrAlo.net/free

Copyright and Permissions

All copyrights are held by Z Media Group LLC (ZMG) and its subsidiaries. As a ZMG customer, you are permitted to print one (1) copy of this book for your own personal use or read it on a digital device if you purchased a digital copy of this book. Such printing may be done by a commercial printer and permission is hereby granted to commercial printers to print this book for the purposes set herein.

You may not email this book or otherwise share it with anyone who has not paid the nominal fee to purchase this book. We have gone out of our way to make this book very affordable and accessible to everyone so that everyone can learn to lose weight properly and benefit from this educational material. The nominal fee helps cover the cost of hosting and delivery of the book to the masses. We take copyright infringements and violations very seriously and will enforce them to the fullest extent of the law. Thank you for your support!

Medical Liability Waiver

I am not your doctor. I do not know you and your medical history personally. I have no idea if you are capable of using the concepts, recipes, and ideas in this book or in any of Dr. Alo's programs ("Dr. Alo's Content"). **Please talk to your doctor and find out if going on a calorie restricted diet and starting an exercise and fitness program is safe for you!**

If you have an eating disorder, you must see a therapist, especially if you can find one that specializes in eating disorders. The advice in this program would not be beneficial for you and may even exacerbate eating disorders. We cannot be held responsible nor liable for any harm that may occur.

It is strongly recommended that you consult with your physician before beginning any exercise program or making any dietary changes or undertaking any other activities described in this book, on our websites, or in any of Dr. Alo's online and mobile platforms, lectures, PowerPoint presentations, books, webinars, videos, seminars, conferences, podcasts, documents, PDF files, worksheets, cheatsheets, guides, and videos owned and operated by Z Media Group, LLC, Dr. Alo, and his subsidiaries ("Dr. Alo's Content"). You need to be in good physical condition to be able to participate in the diet and exercises described in Dr. Alo's Content including both the diet and exercise programs. You must discuss this with your own doctor and specialists that know you and your medical conditions intimately and personally. Specifically, by accepting these terms and proceeding with Dr. Alo's Content you hereby affirm that you have been cleared by your physician(s), are in good physical condition, and do not suffer from any known physical, emotional, psychological, or mental disability or condition which would prevent or limit your participation in dieting, changing eating habits, vigorous physical activity including but not limited to: resistance training, body weight calisthenics, cardiovascular training, jumping, running, stretching, weight lifting, swimming, walking, jogging, etc. You fully understand that you may severely injure yourself as a result of your enrollment and subsequent participation in any book, course or program that Dr. Alo may recommend and you hereby release ZMG and Dr. Alo and his agents from any and all claims or causes of action, known or unknown, now or in the future related to participating in activities or information described in or arising out of Dr. Alo's Content. These conditions may include, but are not limited to, strokes, heart attacks, muscle strains, muscle pulls, muscle tears, broken bones, shin splints, heat prostration, injuries to knees, injuries to back, injuries to foot, or any other illness or soreness that you may incur, including death and other severe illnesses. While Dr. Alo is a fully licensed cardiologist and certified personal trainer, he is not your physician nor your personal trainer. He has not assessed you and knowns nothing about you and your medical conditions. He has no ability to diagnose, examine, or treat any of your medical conditions, or in determining the effect of any specific exercise on a medical condition without a personal assessment and full examination which he does not provide online. The information provided by Dr. Alo is not intended to be a substitute for personalized professional medical advice, diagnosis or treatment. You must be examined by your medical team and personal physician before beginning a new diet or exercise program. After attending workshops, conferences, reading articles, watching videos, listening to podcasts (or video audio) or accessing any of Dr. Alo's Content, you are encouraged to review the information carefully with your own professional healthcare provider and personal physician to determine if this is acceptable and safe for you. Never disregard professional medical advice, or delay in seeking medical advice because of something you have learned from Dr. Alo's Content. Never rely on information in Dr. Alo's Content in place of seeking professional medical advice. Dr. Alo is not your physician and is not familiar with your medical and physical condition.

By continuing this program, you agree to release Dr. Alo and any of his subsidiaries of any and all liability.

Table of Contents

Dedication

Dedicated to my family, friends, and patients who inspired me to write a simple recipe book full of flavorful, heart healthy recipes!

Foreword

Before we get into the meat of this book, I wanted to let you know that you can find even more information, articles, books, videos, resources, and content on https://DrAlo.net

There are online courses that dive deep into weight loss. I also have coaching programs and you can apply to work with me directly at https://DrAlo.net

You can watch all my health related and weight loss related videos on YouTube: http://DrAlo.tv

Why This Book?

The whole idea behind this book is to complement my Actual Weight Loss book. If you have read my Actual Weight Loss book, you will quickly realize that the best way to lose weight is to adhere to a specific calorie count for a long enough period of time. In my weight loss book, we discuss how to calculate the number of calories you need to lose weight. We also emphasize getting enough protein daily to protect lean body mass and make it so you don't lose much muscle in the process.

If you don't have my Actual Weight Loss book, grab it below for a nominal fee or search online retailers for a hard copy.

https://DrAlo.net/book

My Actual Weight Loss book is a great place to start to help you understand why this cookbook was written and how to use it properly and why it will work. I go over all the most important research on weight loss, diet, and exercise.

How to Use This Book

The book is divided up into recipes by calorie counts. If you are on a 2400 calorie diet, you would use the first chapter and eat the breakfast, lunch, dinner, dessert, and snacks in that chapter to lose weight on 2400 calories. The same would go for the 2200, 2000, 1800, 1600, 1400, and 1200 calorie diets. Select that chapter and eat those nutritious and healthy foods to lose weight in a way that is heart healthy, flavorful, and nutritious.

I've designed all these recipes to be heart healthy, flavorful, and nutritious. It's important for healthy food to taste good and be super easy to prepare. You don't want to spend all day in the kitchen. You don't need a PhD to be able to make healthy, tasty food.

I have always made healthy substitutions while cooking food. I try to use olive oil instead of butter for most dishes and use leaner forms of protein for various dishes. You will love my famous turkey chili!

How to Use This Book

The easiest way to calculate your starting calories for weight loss is to multiply your weight by 10. So, if you weigh 200 pounds, you will need to eat 2000 calories to lose weight. You would go to the 2000 calorie chapter and make those foods throughout the day and eat them.

If you weigh 160 pounds, you would jump to the 1600 calorie diet and start there. You should lose weight.

What do you do if you weigh more than 240 pounds and need to eat more than 2400 calories to lose weight? Let's say you weigh 300 pounds and need to eat 3000 or more calories to lose weight properly? You could start with the 2400 calorie diet and just double some of the servings or add some recipes from other chapters that sound good to you. You can also add in my special "Dr. Alo's Protein Packed Smoothie" from the bonus chapter below.

Because protein is important for body composition, satiety, thermic effects, and to preserve muscle mass while dieting down, I have made sure that every chapter provides sufficient protein for most people. There is a bonus tasty protein drink recipe that I have included in the introductory bonus material that provides even more protein. You can substitute one meal per day with this extra yummy protein shake to get 90 grams of protein.

Does the weight x 10 calculation work for everyone? No. But it's a great place to start for most people. If you start on 1800 calories per day and you don't see weight coming off after 3 weeks, you can drop down to the 1600 calorie diet. Wait another 3-4 weeks and see what happens.

If you start gaining weight, then you will need to drop down to the next chapter as well. So, if you are gaining weight on 2200 calories, you need to drop down to the 2000 calorie diet. If you are losing weight too quickly, go up one chapter.

You want to lose about 0.5 to 1.5% of your body weight per week. You don't want to lose it any faster, because then you will risk losing muscle mass. For most people that weight 200 pounds, that's about 1-2 pounds per week. Obviously, as time goes on, and you weigh less, you will not lose weight as quickly.

To preserve muscle mass while dieting, you will need to eat sufficient protein as well as start a strength training program. I highly recommend starting with my simple program that you can download at:

https://DrAlo.net/exercise

If you don't care about preserving muscle mass and just want to lose weight, then don't worry about strength training, and just try to get in enough protein.

Warning:

The 1200 calorie diet is for special cases and likely won't be used by most. Please consult your physician or a registered dietician if you weigh 120 pounds and feel like you need to lose weight. You can still enjoy some of the recipes from that chapter but please only follow a 1200 calorie diet after consultation with your physician or a registered dietician.

If you gain weight when you eat more than 1200 calories, you may need to do something called a reverse diet. It's beyond the scope of this book, grab my Actual Weight Loss book for more info or search YouTube for "Dr. Alo Metabolic Adaptation". Book at https://DrAlo.net/book or search Amazon and Barnes & Noble.

If you have an eating disorder or bad relationship with food, please seek psychiatric help first before starting any food or eating behavior modification program. You need to make sure that this will be ok with you. Read my Actual Weight Loss book for more information on weight loss and developing a

The Healthiest Diet?

The Mediterranean diet is wholesome and nutritious and the only one with research studies showing that it reduces cardiovascular mortality, all-cause mortality, and many types of cancers.

It's a diet based on lean meats, whole grains, lots of fresh fruits and vegetables, beans, legumes, nuts, and olive oil.

You can still eat some foods that are not as wholesome and nutritious, but make sure 80% of your diet is wholesome and nutritious. This will help you with your weight loss goals and will make it easier to adhere to your diet.

But if you don't care and you like Twinkies and other junk food, yes you can lose all the weight you want eating just Twinkies, as long as it adds up to your calorie limit. See my Actual Weight Loss book for more research on this topic. https://DrAlo.net/book or search YouTube for "Dr. Alo Twinkie Diet".

Here's one of many studies showing benefits to a Mediterranean style diet.

BMC Med. 2014 Jul 24;12:112. doi: 10.1186/1741-7015-12-112.

Definitions and potential health benefits of the Mediterranean diet: views from experts around the world.

Trichopoulou A[1], Martínez-González MA, Tong TY, Forouhi NG, Khandelwal S, Prabhakaran D, Mozaffarian D, de Lorgeril M.

⊕ Author information

Abstract

The Mediterranean diet has been linked to a number of health benefits, including reduced mortality risk and lower incidence of cardiovascular dis Definitions of the Mediterranean diet vary across some settings, and scores are increasingly being employed to define Mediterranean diet adhere in epidemiological studies. Some components of the Mediterranean diet overlap with other healthy dietary patterns, whereas other aspects are ur to the Mediterranean diet. In this forum article, we asked clinicians and researchers with an interest in the effect of diet on health to describe wha constitutes a Mediterranean diet in different geographical settings, and how we can study the health benefits of this dietary pattern.

And another showing reduction in new cancers and overall mortality.

\theroscler Rep. 2013 Dec;15(12):370. doi: 10.1007/s11883-013-0370-4.

literranean diet and cardiovascular disease: historical perspective and latest evidence.

rgeril M.

ıthor information

:ract

:oncept that the Mediterranean diet was associated with a lower incidence of cardiovascular disease (CVD) was first proposed in the 1950s. ₂ then, there have been randomized controlled trials and large epidemiological studies that reported associations with lower CVD: in 1994 and , the reports of the intermediate and final analyses of the trial Lyon Diet Heart Study; in 2003, a major epidemiological study in Greece showing a g inverse association between a Mediterranean score and the risk of cardiovascular complications; in 2011-2012, several reports showing that non-Mediterranean populations can gain benefits from long-term adhesion to the Mediterranean diet; and in 2013, the PREDIMED trial showing ıificant risk reduction in a low-risk population. Contrary to the pharmacological approach of cardiovascular prevention, the adoption of the terranean diet has been associated with a significant reduction in new cancers and overall mortality. Thus, in terms of evidence-based medicine, ıll adoption of a modern version of the Mediterranean diet pattern can be considered one of the most effective approaches for the prevention of and nonfatal CVD complications.

24105622 [PubMed - indexed for MEDLINE]

And yes, all your cardiovascular markers improve regardless of what macronutrients you eat, as long as weight is coming off. It's the weight loss alone that confers protection. Take a look at the studies below. It doesn't matter if you eat mostly fat, mostly carbs, no carbs, some protein, no protein… as long as you are in a calorie deficit, and you are losing weight, you will improve all of your cardiovascular markers!

Changes in weight loss, body composition and cardiovascular disease risk after altering macronutrient distributions during a regular exercise program in obese women

Chad M Kerksick, Jennifer Wismann-Bunn, Donovan Fogt, Ashli R Thomas, Lem Taylor, Bill I Campbell, Colin D Wilborn, Travis Harvey, Mike D Roberts, Paul La Bounty, Melyn Galbreath, Brandon Marcello, Christopher J Rasmussen & Richard B Kreider

Background

This study's purpose investigated the impact of different macronutrient distributions and varying caloric intakes along with regular exercise for metabolic and physiological changes related to weight loss.

Methods

One hundred forty-one sedentary, obese women (38.7 ± 8.0 yrs, 163.3 ± 6.9 cm, 93.2 ± 16.5 kg, 35.0 ± 6.2 kg·m^{-2}, 44.8 ± 4.2% fat) were randomized to either diet + no exercise control group (CON) a no diet + exercise control (ND), or one of four diet + exercise groups (high-energy diet [HED], very low carbohydrate high protein diet [VLCHP], low carbohydrate, moderate protein diet [LCMP] and high carbohydrate, low protein [HCLP]) in addition to beginning a 3x·week[1] supervised resistance training program. After 0, 1, 10 and 14 weeks, all participants completed testing sessions which included anthropometric, body composition, energy expenditure, fasting blood samples, aerobic and muscular fitness assessments. Data were analyzed using repeated measures ANOVA with an alpha of 0.05 with LSD post-hoc analysis when appropriate.

Results

All dieting groups exhibited adequate compliance to their prescribed diet regimen as energy and macronutrient amounts and distributions were close to prescribed amounts. Those groups that followed a diet and exercise program reported significantly greater anthropometric (waist circumference and body ma and body composition via DXA (fat mass and % fat) changes. Caloric restriction initially reduced energy expenditure, but successfully returned to baseline values after 10 weeks of dieting and exercising. Significant fitness improvements (aerobic capacity and maximal strength) occurred in all exercising groups. N significant changes occurred in lipid panel constituents, but serum insulin and HOMA-IR values decreased in the VLCHP group. Significant reductions in ser leptin occurred in all caloric restriction + exercise groups after 14 weeks, which were unchanged in other non-diet/non-exercise groups.

Conclusions

Overall and over the entire test period, all diet groups which restricted their caloric intake and exercised experienced similar responses to each other. Regular exercise and modest caloric restriction successfully promoted anthropometric and body composition improvements along with various markers of muscular fitness. Significant increases in relative energy expenditure and reductions in circulating leptin were found in response to all exercise and diet groups. Macronutrient distribution may impact circulating levels of insulin and overall ability to improve strength levels in obese women who follow regular exercise.

Regardless of what macronutrient breakdown you use, if you are losing weight, all of your cardiovascular risk factors improve

Take a look at another study (below) that was published in the New England Journal of Medicine. Regardless of which macronutrient you emphasize, your cardiovascular markers will all improve, so long as the diet you are following is actually causing weight loss.

J Med. Author manuscript; available in PMC 2009 Oct 19.

://www.ncbi.nlm.nih.gov/pmc/73.
es/PMC2763382/
Click to follow link
19246357

mparison of Weight-Loss Diets with Different Compositions of Fat, Protein, and rbohydrates

M. Sacks, M.D.,[1,2] George A. Bray, M.D.,[5] Vincent J. Carey, Ph.D.,[2] Steven R. Smith, M.D.,[5] Donna H. Ryan, M.D.,[5]
en D. Anton, Ph.D.,[5] Katherine McManus, M.S., R.D.,[4] Catherine M. Champagne, Ph.D.,[5] Louise M. Bishop, M.S., R.D.,[1] Nancy Laranjo, B.A.,[2] Meryl S. Leboff, M.D.,[3]
fer C. Rood, Ph.D.,[5] Lilian de Jonge, Ph.D.,[5] Frank L. Greenway, M.D.,[5] Catherine M. Loria, Ph.D.,[6] Eva Obarzanek, Ph.D.,[6] and Donald A. Williamson, Ph.D.[5]
r information Copyright and License information Disclaimer

ublisher's final edited version of this article is available at N Engl J Med
ther articles in PMC that cite the published article.

ciated Data
lementary Materials

act

KGROUND
ossible advantage for weight loss of a diet that emphasizes protein, fat, or carbohydrates has not been established, and there are few studies that extend beyond 1 year.

HODS
andomly assigned 811 overweight adults to one of four diets; the targeted percentages of energy derived from fat, protein, and carbohydrates in the four diets were 20, 15, 5%; 20, 25, and 55%; 40, 15, and 45%; and 40, 25, and 35%. The diets consisted of similar foods and met guidelines for cardiovascular health. The participants were d group and individual instructional sessions for 2 years. The primary outcome was the change in body weight after 2 years in two-by-two factorial comparisons of low fat s high fat and average protein versus high protein and in the comparison of highest and lowest carbohydrate content.

JLTS
nonths, participants assigned to each diet had lost an average of 6 kg, which represented 7% of their initial weight; they began to regain weight after 12 months. By 2 years, t loss remained similar in those who were assigned to a diet with 15% protein and those assigned to a diet with 25% protein (3.0 and 3.6 kg, respectively); in those ned to a diet with 20% fat and those assigned to a diet with 40% fat (3.3 kg for both groups); and in those assigned to a diet with 65% carbohydrates and those assigned to : with 35% carbohydrates (2.9 and 3.4 kg, respectively) (P>0.20 for all comparisons). Among the 80% of participants who completed the trial, the average weight loss was 4 t to 15% of the participants had a reduction of at least 10% of their initial body weight. Satiety, hunger, satisfaction with the diet, and attendance at group sessions were r for all diets; attendance was strongly associated with weight loss (0.2 kg per session attended). The diets improved lipid-related risk factors and fasting insulin levels.

CLUSIONS
ced-calorie diets result in clinically meaningful weight loss regardless of which macronutrients they emphasize.

Conclusions on diet and cardiovascular risk:
- Obesity and elevated BMI increase all inflammatory and cardiovascular risk factors
- Calorie deficit and weight loss improve all cardiovascular risk factors
- Macronutrient breakdown makes no difference
- Leaner individuals have less cardiovascular and all-cause mortality risk

If you want all the science and research studies behind all my diet and weight loss strategies, I highly recommend you grab my Actual Weight Loss book.

https://DrAlo.net/book

Bonus Chapter

I've also decided to include some of my family's favorite recipes. My parents immigrated to the United States in the mid-70s and brought with them their own unique palate, spices, and flavors from Syria. My mother had to adapt a lot of her dishes to make them healthier over the years and they still taste amazing! Some would say that they taste even better. Two of her boys are cardiologists, so she kind of had to adapt. Growing up in small Midwestern towns while eating a Mideastern cuisine was invigorating. In grade school, many of my friends would look at my lunch and ask, "What is that?" I would try to explain unsuccessfully. Middle Eastern cuisine is so popular in Ohio now that I rarely need explain what I am eating or making.

The family recipes are bonuses! If you are feeling adventurous one day, use one instead of your other dishes. You won't be disappointed!

Many of my family's favorite recipes are now standard Americana; Hummus, Lentil soup, Taboulah, and many others!

Want more recipes, tips, tricks, and weight loss secrets? The website is always being updated!

http://DrAlo.net/free

Special Thanks to Sahra Peshimam for helping edit this book! I'm eternally grateful!

Bonus Recipe:
Dr. Alo's Protein Packed Smoothie

3 scoops Optimum Nutrition Whey Protein Isolate
Strawberry Delicious
4 oz frozen berry mix
3/4 cup (170g) Fage 0% Greek Yogurt
Water to top it off
Mint and fresh berries for garnish
1 packet of Splenda (optional)

Blend in blender until smooth, pour into glass.
Top with berries and fresh mint. Drink!

Nutrition Facts	
Servings: 1	
Amount per serving	
Calories	450
	%Daily Value*
Total Fat 3g	8%
Sodium 65mg	13%
Total Carbohydrate 16g	16%
Protein 90g	

Use this as a meal replacement for any meal in the following chapters to give you a very tasty, protein packed meal. This will ensure that you are hitting your protein targets.

2400
Calories

175g
Protein

284g
Carbs

98g
Fat

Meal Plan

BREAKFAST:
Kodiak Cakes Protein Pancakes
Prep Time: 10m   Cook Time: 5m   Total Time: 15m

1/2 medium banana
1 cup Fage 0% Greek yogurt
1 egg
2oz frozen blueberry, (half as is other half mashed with juice)
½ cup Kodiak Cakes pancake mix
1 scoop of Optimum Nutrition vanilla protein powder
4 tbsp water

In a medium bowl, mash the banana with a fork until almost liquid. Add the yogurt, egg, blueberries with juice, pancake mix and water. Mix well. Heat a nonstick griddle or frying pan over medium-high heat. Grease the pan with non-stick spray to keep the pancakes from sticking. Using a ladle, pour small circles of batter in the pan. Cook for a few minutes, until bubbles from on top of the pancakes. Flip the pancakes and cook until firm.

Nutrition Facts	
Servings: 1	
Amount per serving	
Calories	**516**
	%Daily Value*
Total Fat 7g	**9%**
Sodium 523mg	**23%**
Total Carbohydrate 52g	**19%**
Protein 65g	

15

LUNCH:
Organic Chicken Barley Salad

Prep Time: 20m Cook Time: 20m   Total Time: 40m

5oz boneless, skinless chicken breasts
25g barley
½ cups no sodium (or low sodium) chicken broth
1/2 lemon - zest and juice
1 tbsp olive oil
1 tsp chopped fresh oregano
1 tsp chopped fresh dill
2 tsp chopped fresh parsley
1 head red-leaf lettuce, chopped
1 tbsp red onion, sliced
55g cherry tomatoes, sliced
1/2 avocados, sliced
Kosher salt and freshly ground black pepper
1 tbsp whole-grain mustard
1 tsp dried oregano
⅓ cup extra-virgin olive oil
Kosher salt and freshly ground black pepper

Nutrition Facts	
Servings: 1	
Amount per serving	
Calories	**685**
	%Daily Value*
Total Fat 44g	**55%**
Sodium 488mg	**21%**
Total Carbohydrate 42g	**15%**
Protein 44g	

16

Start by marinating the chicken in olive oil, lemon zest, lemon juice, oregano, dill and parsley and refrigerate for 30 minutes.

In the meantime, in a medium pan, place the grain and chicken stock to stew over medium heat. When it simmers, cover the pot and cook until the grain is totally cooked, 35 to 45 minutes. Sieve and save.

In a medium bowl, whisk together the lemon zest, lemon juice, mustard, and oregano. Slowly stream in the olive oil (same way you make mayonnaise, or it will separate), and whisk well. Season with salt and pepper.

Set your grill on high. Take out the chicken from the marinade and season with salt and pepper.

Grill the chicken until seared on both sides and completely cooked through.

In a large bowl, plate the lettuce, onion, tomatoes, grain, and dressing. Slice the chicken and serve on top of the plate of mixed greens top with the avocado.

DINNER:
Quinoa Labneh
Prep Time: 10m **Cook Time:** 40m **Total Time:** 50m

185g quinoa, rinsed
20g cherry tomatoes, sliced in half
10g eggplant, cubed
10g zucchini, cubed
25g Romano beans (or green beans)
1 tbsp extra-virgin olive oil
Kosher salt and freshly ground black pepper
45g of your favorite pesto (either homemade or store bought)
61g of labneh or Fage 0% Greek yogurt
1/2 garlic clove, minced
Juice from ½ lemon
Handful of cilantro or parsley (or both!), roughly chopped

Nutrition Facts	
Servings: 1	
Amount per serving	
Calories	**863**
	%Daily Value*
Total Fat 45g	**57%**
Sodium 321mg	**14%**
Total Carbohydrate 129g	**47%**
Protein 18g	

Preheat the oven to 400°F. Line a large baking sheet with parchment paper and arrange the eggplant, zucchini, cherry tomatoes and beans on it. Drizzle the olive oil over the veggies and season with salt and pepper. Roast until all of the veggies are tender and caramelized, 30 to 40 minutes.

Meanwhile, add the quinoa to a medium saucepan with 2 cups of water and a pinch of salt. Bring to a boil, cover, reduce to a simmer and cook for 15 minutes. Once the quinoa is done cooking, remove the lid, fluff with a fork, and allow to cool. Once the quinoa has cooled slightly, toss it with the pesto.

Mix the labneh, garlic, lemon juice and herbs together in a small bowl.

Assemble each bowl by adding quinoa and arranging the veggies in rows to look like a rainbow. Then add a dollop of the labneh on the side.

DESSERT:
Dry Fig Yogurt
Prep Time: 2m Cook Time: 2m   Total Time: 4m

227g (1 cup) Fage 0% Greek yogurt
3 dried figs, sliced
2 tsp honey
1 scoop Optimum Nutrition Vanilla whey protein

Mix all ingredient together and enjoy!!

Nutrition Facts	
Servings: 1	
Amount per serving	
Calories	**438**
	%Daily Value*
Total Fat 2g	**3%**
Sodium 168mg	**7%**
Total Carbohydrate 61g	**22%**
Protein 48g	

2200
Calories

114g
Protein

180g
Carbs

114g
Fat

Meal Plan

BREAKFAST:
Yogurt, Tomato Salsa, Pickled Onions, Poached egg

Prep Time: 10m   Cook Time: 20m   Total Time: 30m

227g (1 cup) of Fage 0% Greek yogurt
3 tbsp of Mexican tomato sauce
1 roma tomato
1 red pepper
1 garlic clove
Half a red onion
1 tbsp balsamic vinegar
2 poached eggs
Side of crackers
1 tsp Olive oil
Pinch of salt & ground pepper
Herbs (thyme, oregano, sage, rosemary, or your favorites)

Nutrition Facts	
Servings: 1	
Amount per serving	
Calories	**434**
	%Daily Value*
Total Fat 16g	**20%**
Sodium 479mg	**21%**
Total Carbohydrate 37g	**13%**
Protein 41g	

Tomato Salsa: In a baking pan, place a baking sheet and place on it: the tomato, red pepper, garlic, red onion, sprinkle some aromatic herbs (thyme, oregano, sage, rosemary) and a drizzle of olive oil before grilling them in a preheated oven.

Once cooked, place them in a blender adding half a tablespoon of balsamic vinegar, a tablespoon of olive oil, salt, and fresh ground black pepper, blending them into a combined red sauce.

Place the Greek yogurt in a bowl.

In a deep saucepan, place 250 ml of water and ¼ tsp of salt and bring them to boil before cracking 2 eggs and cooking them in the water till the whites are completely cooked.

Remove the eggs from the water and place them over the yogurt mix.

Drizzle 3 tbsp of salsa over the eggs.

Sprinkle some black pepper and a small pinch of salt before finishing with a drizzle of olive oil. Served with a side of toasted bread or pita bread

LUNCH:
Eggplant Marinara

Prep Time: 15m   Cook Time: 20m   Total Time: 35m

50g eggplants
3 tbsp olive oil
74g marinara sauce
56g shredded low fat mozzarella cheese
49g cherry tomatoes, halved
½ cup torn basil leaves

Nutrition Facts	
Servings: 1	
Amount per serving	
Calories	**606**
	%Daily Value*
Total Fat 56g	**72%**
Sodium 647mg	**28%**
Total Carbohydrate 17g	**6%**
Protein 1g	

Preheat the oven to 400°F. Prepare a baking tray with parchment paper.

Cut the eggplant(s) into ¾ inch thick slices. Arrange the eggplant and brush both sides of each slice with olive oil. Season with salt and pepper.

Roast the eggplant slices until nearly tender, about 10 to 12 minutes.

Remove the tray from the oven and spread 2 tablespoons marinara sauce on top of each piece. Top generously with mozzarella and arrange 3 to 5 cherry tomato pieces on top of each.

Return the slices to the oven and roast until the cheese is melted and the tomatoes are blistered, about 5 to 7 minutes.

Serve hot garnished with basil.

DINNER:
Easy Peasy Chickpea and Chicken Bowl

Prep Time: 10m Cook Time: 10m   Total Time: 20m

164g canned chickpeas, rinsed and drained
170g cooked chicken breast, in bite-sized pieces
60g lettuce, chopped
74g cherry tomatoes, halved
10g bell pepper, chopped
1 scallion, thinly chopped
1 garlic clove, minced
30g olives
1 tbsp feta cheese, crumbled
Juice of ½ lemon
20g parsley, thinly chopped
Black pepper & salt
1 tbsp olive oil

Place all ingredients into a bowl. Mix until combined and add salt and pepper to taste.

Nutrition Facts	
Servings: 1	
Amount per serving	
Calories	**900**
	%Daily Value*
Total Fat 31g	**40%**
Sodium 465mg	**20%**
Total Carbohydrate 111g	**40%**
Protein 50g	

DESSERT:
Cheesy Apple Parfait
Prep Time: 15m Cook Time: 35m Total Time: 50m

2 large apples, peeled, cored, and diced
1/4 teaspoon cinnamon
3 tablespoons blonde coconut sugar
1 pinch of sea salt
2/3 cup fat-free cream cheese softened
1/3 cup Fage 0% Greek yogurt
4 dates no sugar added
1/2 cup walnut halves (about 18)

Nutrition Facts	
Servings: 8	
Amount per serving	
Calories	**172**
	%Daily Value*
Total Fat 11g	**15%**
Sodium 92mg	**4%**
Total Carbohydrate 15g	**6%**
Protein 4g	

Add diced apples, 1 teaspoon coconut sugar, salt, and cinnamon to a medium pot. Cover and cook on medium heat until apples begin to boil. Reduce heat to a simmer and cook until tender, approximately 30 minutes. Be careful not to turn into applesauce. Allow to cool to room temperature before adding to dessert dishes.

While apples are cooking, in a medium mixing bowl, add softened cream cheese, yogurt, and remaining coconut sugar. Beat with an electric mixer until smooth and sugar is dissolved (about 2 minutes). Refrigerate until ready to use.

Add dates to a food processor and pulse until finely diced. Add walnuts and continue to pulse until it's a coarse crumb consistency and well combined with dates.

Evenly layer on each dessert dish the walnut mixture, cream cheese, and lastly cooked apples. Sprinkle any remaining walnut mixture over the top.

Refrigerate until ready to serve.

2000
Calories

154g
Protein

162g
Carbs

115g
Fat

Meal Plan

BREAKFAST:
Eggs, Feta and Arugula Open Face Sandwich

Prep Time: 5m   Cook Time: 5m   Total Time: 10m

4 oz (100g) Feta cheese mashed with olive oil into a paste consistency
80g arugula leaves (or dandelion)
1 red pepper medium size finely diced
1 clove of garlic finely minced
3 eggs
One slice of Dave's Killer Bread 21 Whole Grain Thin Sliced
Olive oil
Pinch of salt
Pinch of fresh ground black pepper

Nutrition Facts	
Servings: 1	
Amount per serving	
Calories	607
	%Daily Value*
Total Fat 42g	53%
Sodium 211mg	92%
Total Carbohydrate 50g	18%
Protein 36g	

In a pan, drizzle one tbsp of olive oil. Toss in the minced garlic and finely chopped red pepper. Sauté for 1 min.

In a separate bowl, crack 3 eggs and beat them heavily. Add the beaten eggs to the pan with the garlic and minced red pepper.

Add the salt and black pepper and stir them to get a scrambled eggs consistency without overcooking them and remove from heat.

Drizzle a bit of olive oil on the slice of bread and place it in a 350-degree preheated oven for 5 min.

Spread the feta cheese on the toasted sour dough.

Add the scrambled eggs on top of the cheese.

Finely chop the dandelions and sprinkle them on the eggs.

Finish with a drizzle of olive oil.

LUNCH:
Arugula Chicken Salad
Prep Time: 10m   Chill Time: 30m   Total Time: 40m

170g chicken breast marinated in the juices of half a lemon, a sprinkle of oregano, salt and pepper
10g canned white beans
40g avocado
50g walnuts
4 cherry tomatoes cut in half
1/2 bunch of arugula leaves
Juice of 1/2 lemon
1/2 tsp of yellow mustard
1 tsp of olive oil
Salt and pepper
35g grated Halloumi cheese (or goat cheese)

Nutrition Facts	
Servings: 1	
Amount per serving	
Calories	673
	%Daily Value*
Total Fat 47g	**60%**
Sodium 131mg	**6%**
Total Carbohydrate 16g	**6%**
Protein 52g	

Add a tbsp of olive oil in a pan and place on a medium heat and sear the marinated chicken breast on both sides before covering the pan and lowering the heat until fully cooked. Place the chicken aside for later.

In a bowl, layer the arugula leaves, diced avocados, cherry tomatoes and roughly place the white bean all around.

In a blender, blend the mustard, lemon juice, and the olive oil with some salt and pepper. Drizzle them on the salad mix along with the grated halloumi cheese.

Slice the cooled chicken breast and place it on top.

DINNER:
Scampi & Calamari in Tomato Sauce

Prep Time: 5m   Cook Time: 15m   Total Time: 20m

125g (about 10 large shrimp) shrimp (peeled)
60g calamari
1 tomato – cubed
1 garlic clove
5 leaves basil – chopped
1 tbsp tomato paste
1 tsp olive oil
1 slice Dave's Killer Bread 21 Whole Grain Thin Sliced

Nutrition Facts	
Servings: 1	
Amount per serving	
Calories	**535**
	%Daily Value*
Total Fat 17g	**23%**
Sodium 435mg	**45%**
Total Carbohydrate 41g	**15%**
Protein 52g	

Dice the tomatoes. Clean and cut calamari in strips. Wash and chop basil. Clean shrimp.
In a large non-stick skillet place chopped tomatoes and calamari and cover with a lid.
Cook at medium high heat for 5 minutes, but be sure to check occasionally to see if there is enough sauce in the pan.

After 5 minutes, uncover, add tomato paste, stir it in well, until you see the sauce thicken up.
Add shrimp and garlic and stir. Let it cook like this for 2-3 min.
If the sauce gets too runny – add a bit more tomato paste.
Then add basil, stir for 1 min. Turn off heat. Add olive oil and serve with Dave's bread.

BREAKFAST:
Pear On Sourdough

Prep Time: 5m Cook Time: 5m   Total Time: 10m

1 Pear
100g of ricotta cheese (3.5 ounces)
1 tbsp of honey
5 leaves of finely chopped mint leaves
One slice of sour dough bread

Using a mandolin, finely slice the halved pear after deseeding it.
Drizzle a bit of olive oil on the sour dough slice and place it for 5 min in a preheated oven on 400°F until slightly toasted. Spread the ricotta cheese on the toast. Add the sliced pear on top
Drizzle the honey on the sandwich.
Garnish with roughly chopped mint.

Nutrition Facts	
Servings: 1	
Amount per serving	
Calories	**340**
	%Daily Value*
Total Fat 9g	**11%**
Sodium 258mg	**11%**
Total Carbohydrate 55g	**20%**
Protein 14g	

1800
Calories

153g
Protein

153g
Carbs

111g
Fat

Meal Plan

BREAKFAST:
Dr. Alo's Killer Avocado Toast

Prep Time: 5m   **Cook Time:** 5m   **Total Time:** 10m

1 slice Dave's Killer Bread 21 Whole Grain Thin Sliced
½ medium avocado mashed
Zest and juice of half a lime
4oz smoked salmon (no or low sodium, can use non smoked salmon as well)
1oz red onion sliced thinly
Pinch of chili pepper
2 eggs
Wild arugula

Nutrition Facts	
Servings: 1	
Amount per serving	
Calories	**351**
	%Daily Value*
Total Fat 35g	**45%**
Sodium 2505mg	**109%**
Total Carbohydrate 24g	**9%**
Protein 38g	

Start by heating the toast in an oven for 2 min at 400 degrees (or use toaster).
In a bowl, mash the avocado with a fork. Mix in the onion, lime juice and zest, and chili flakes.
Prepare the poached eggs by adding 2 freshly cracked eggs to boiling water until the white is totally cooked.
Spread the avocado mix on top of the toast, add the salmon slice topped with 2 poached eggs and sprinkle couple leaves of wild arugula.

LUNCH:
Chicken Artichoke

Prep Time: 20m Cook Time: 45m Total Time: 1h5m

2 medium sized artichoke hearts
100ml of chicken stock (about 7 ounces)
50ml of water (4.5 ounces)
90g finely chopped chicken breast
5g of finely chopped parsley
1/2 finely chopped small tomato
1/2 finely chopped small onions
1/2 finely chopped garlic glove
3 halved cherry tomatoes
1/2 cup breadcrumbs
Juices of 1 lemon
2 tbsp of Olive oil
Salt and pepper

Nutrition Facts	
Servings: 1	
Amount per serving	
Calories	627
	%Daily Value*
Total Fat 34g	**44%**
Sodium 815mg	**35%**
Total Carbohydrate 53g	**19%**
Protein 30g	

In a frying pan, add olive oil and sear the finely chopped chicken breast, onion, and garlic until they are cooked. Then add the tomatoes to the mix and cook them together. Then add the breadcrumbs and set aside.

In a casserole dish, place the artichoke hearts, in rows and top with the chicken mix.

Cover with chicken stock & water. Bake at 350 degrees for 25 minutes. Salt and pepper to taste after done baking.

Once cooked, remove from the heat squeeze lemon juice and sprinkle chopped parsley on top.

DINNER:
Salmon Tartin

Prep Time: 5m   Cook Time: 10m   Total Time: 15m

6oz of fresh salmon
One slice of Dave's Killer Bread 21 Whole Grain Thin Sliced
2oz of chopped celery
Juice of 1 lemon
2 tbsp of olive oil
Salt and pepper
10g fresh grapefruit, sectioned

In a 350°F preheated oven, place the bread slice drizzled with some olive oil and toast it. Pan fry the salmon in a hot pan with olive oil until pink from the inside.
Place the bread in a serving plate, align the salmon, drizzle the chopped celery on top, slices of grapefruit and drizzle a line of olive oil, add a pinch of salt and pepper to taste

Nutrition Facts	
Servings: 1	
Amount per serving	
Calories	437
	%Daily Value*
Total Fat 40g	51%
Sodium 220mg	10%
Total Carbohydrate 15g	5%
Protein 37g	

DESSERT:
Dry Fig Yogurt
Prep Time: 2m   Cook Time: 2m   Total Time: 4m

227g (1 cup) Fage 0% Greek yogurt
3 dried figs, sliced
2 tsp honey
1 scoop Optimum Nutrition Vanilla whey protein

Mix all ingredient together and enjoy!

Nutrition Facts	
Servings: 1	
Amount per serving	
Calories	**438**
	%Daily Value*
Total Fat 2g	**3%**
Sodium 168mg	**7%**
Total Carbohydrate 61g	**22%**
Protein 48g	

1600
Calories

106g
Protein

111g
Carbs

86g
Fat

Meal Plan

BREAKFAST:
Chia Barley Breakfast Mix
Prep Time: 5m   Cook Time: 5m   Total Time: 10m

15g old-fashioned rolled oats
17g barley flakes
15g quinoa
13g dried fruit, such as raisins, cranberries and/or chopped apricots
10g chia
½ tsp ground cinnamon
¾ tsp salt

Mix all with 1 1/4 cups water in a small saucepan. Bring to a boil. Reduce heat, partially cover and simmer, stirring occasionally, until thickened, 12 to 15 minutes. Let stand, covered, for 5 minutes. Add sweetener of your choice and top with more dried fruit, if desired.

Nutrition Facts	
Servings: 1	
Amount per serving	
Calories	**257**
	%Daily Value*
Total Fat 5g	**7%**
Sodium 806mg	**79%**
Total Carbohydrate 47g	**17%**
Protein 8g	

LUNCH:
Greek Salad

Prep Time: 10m Cook Time: 10m Total Time: 20m

Dressing:
1 tbsp olive oil
1 tsp red wine vinegar
1 tsp balsamic vinegar
1 tsp of the feta brine
1 tsp fresh dill, chopped
2g dried oregano
¼ tsp sea salt
1 clove garlic, very finely minced
Juice from ½ lemon
6oz grilled chicken breast

Greek Salad:
1/2 bell peppers, chopped
½ cucumber, chopped
10g cherry or grape tomatoes, cut in half
¼ small red onion, thinly sliced
50g feta cheese, crumbled or cut into small pieces
20g pitted kalamata olives

Nutrition Facts	
Servings: 1	
Amount per serving	
Calories	**553**
	%Daily Value*
Total Fat 34g	**43%**
Sodium 295mg	**56%**
Total Carbohydrate 19g	**7%**
Protein 46g	

Start with the dressing: mix the olive oil, both vinegars, feta brine, dill, oregano, sea salt, garlic, and lemon juice in a medium-sized bowl.
Add all chopped veggies in a bowl topped with feta cheese and olives. Pour the dressing over the top and toss to coat.

DINNER:
Open Face Chicken Sandwich

Prep Time: 10m   Chill Time: 30m   Total Time: 40m

170g chicken breast
1 lemon
1tsp oregano
15g watercress
½ sliced green apple
One small finely chopped pickled onions
One slice of Dave's Killer Bread 21 Whole Grain Thin Sliced
1/2 avocado mashed with salt, pepper and olive oil

Add a tbsp of olive oil in a pan and place on a medium heat and sear the chicken breast on both sides before covering the pan, adding oregano, and lowering the heat to fully cook. Rest the chicken aside until it cools off.
Spread the avocado mash over the slice of bread. Layer with the sliced apple topped with watercress and the finely chopped onions.

Nutrition Facts	
Servings: 1	
Amount per serving	
Calories	**538**
	%Daily Value*
Total Fat 27g	**35%**
Sodium 282mg	**12%**
Total Carbohydrate 32g	**12%**
Protein 44g	

SNACK:
Green Dip

Prep Time: 10m   Cook Time: 5m Total Time: 15m

½ large avocado
½ cup edamame beans
3 tbsp tahini (sesame paste, can be found in Middle East markets)
2 large cloves garlic
Juice of ½ lemon
A handful of fresh cilantro (stems and leaves)
½ tsp cumin
Salt and pepper to taste
2 to 3 tbsp water

Pulse all ingredients together in a food processor. Add water 1 tbsp. at a time to desired consistency. Serve with salty crackers

Nutrition Facts	
Servings: 3	
Amount per serving	
Calories	239
	%Daily Value*
Total Fat 19g	25%
Sodium 26mg	1%
Total Carbohydrate 13g	5%
Protein 8g	

1400
Calories

69g
Protein

172g
Carbs

60g
Fat

Meal Plan

BREAKFAST:
Sour Sweet Potato

Prep Time: 5m Cook Time: 20m Total Time: 25m

1 medium sized sweet potato
1 tsp of sumac
1 tsp of oregano
1/2 finely chopped garlic
2 tbsp of Fage 0% Greek yogurt
Olive oil
Salt and pepper

After peeling and washing the potatoes, cut them in halves the longways and place them in a baking sheet. Add the oregano, the olive oil, the chopped garlic, a pinch of salt and pepper, and bake them in a preheated 350°F oven for 45 min.

In the serving plate, place the cooked potatoes, sprinkle the sumac on top and finish with one tbsp of Fage 0% over each piece of potato.

Nutrition Facts	
Servings: 1	
Amount per serving	
Calories	179
	%Daily Value*
Total Fat 5g	6%
Sodium 19mg	1%
Total Carbohydrate 30g	11%
Protein 4g	

LUNCH:
Salmon Tartin
Prep Time: 5m Cook Time: 10m Total Time: 15m

6oz of fresh salmon
One slice of Dave's Killer Bread 21 Whole Grain
Thin Sliced
2oz of chopped celery
Juice of 1 lemon
2 tbsp of olive oil
Salt and pepper
10g fresh grapefruit, sectioned

In a 180°C preheated oven, place the bread slice drizzled with some olive oil and toast it. Pan fry the salmon in a hot pan with olive oil until pink from the inside.
Place the bread in a serving plate, align the salmon, drizzle the chopped celery on top, slices of grapefruit and drizzle a line of olive oil, add a pinch of salt and pepper to taste

Nutrition Facts	
Servings: 1	
Amount per serving	
Calories	437
	%Daily Value*
Total Fat 40g	**51%**
Sodium 220mg	**10%**
Total Carbohydrate 15g	**5%**
Protein 37g	

DINNER:
Al Portobello

Prep Time: 5m   Cook Time: 20m   Total Time: 25m

1 portobello mushroom
60g of breadcrumbs
5g of chopped parsley
1/3 finely chopped garlic
30g of low-fat shredded mozzarella
1 tsp of olive oil
Chili powder
Salt and pepper

In a bowl, add the breadcrumbs, the parsley, the chopped garlic, the shredded mozzarella and mix them together with a sprinkle of chili powder.
Stuff the portobello mushroom with the above mixture and drizzle with olive oil. Sprinkle with salt and pepper.
Place the portobello on an oven tray and cook it in a preheated oven over 200°C for 20 min. Serve warm.

Nutrition Facts	
Servings: 1	
Amount per serving	
Calories	326
	%Daily Value*
Total Fat 9g	12%
Sodium 506mg	22%
Total Carbohydrate 48g	17%
Protein 14g	

DESSERT:
Ricotta Peach Toast
Prep Time: 5m   Cook Time: 5m   Total Time: 10m

1 tbsp part-skim ricotta cheese (or Fage 0% Greek yogurt)
1 tsp honey, divided
⅛ tsp cinnamon
1 slice Dave's Killer Bread 21 Whole Grain Thin Sliced toasted
½ medium peach, sliced
1 tbsp chopped pistachios

Combine ricotta, ½ teaspoon honey and cinnamon in a small bowl.

Spread the ricotta mixture on toast and top with peach and pistachios. Drizzle with the remaining 1/2 teaspoon honey.

Nutrition Facts	
Servings: 1	
Amount per serving	
Calories	417
	%Daily Value*
Total Fat 6g	8%
Sodium 360mg	16%
Total Carbohydrate 79g	29%
Protein 14g	

1200
Calories

83g
Protein

113g
Carbs

65g
Fat

Meal Plan

BREAKFAST:
Poached Egg Artichoke Toast

Prep Time: 5m Cook Time: 10m Total Time: 15m

1 tsp extra-virgin olive oil
½ cup finely chopped artichoke hearts
1 sliced scallion
¼ tsp dried oregano
⅛ tsp ground pepper
1 slice whole-wheat bread, toasted
2 large eggs poached

Heat oil in a small skillet. Add all ingredients and sauté until hot for 1-2 minutes. Spread on toast and top with poached eggs.

Nutrition Facts	
Servings: 1	
Amount per serving	
Calories	**297**
	%Daily Value*
Total Fat 16g	**20%**
Sodium 344mg	**15%**
Total Carbohydrate 23g	**8%**
Protein 19g	

LUNCH:
Eggplant Rolls

Prep Time: 10m   Cook Time: 30m   Total Time: 40m

1/2 medium eggplants, halved
1 tablespoons olive oil, divided
1/2 red onion, diced
1 garlic clove, minced
25g of white mushrooms, quartered
33g chopped kale
40g cooked quinoa
1 tsp chopped fresh thyme
Zest and juice of 1 lemon (plus additional lemon wedges for serving)
Salt and fresh ground black pepper
30g Fage 0% Greek yogurt
1 tsp chopped fresh parsley, for garnish

Nutrition Facts	
Servings: 1	
Amount per serving	
Calories	423
	%Daily Value*
Total Fat 18g	**23%**
Sodium 149mg	**2%**
Total Carbohydrate 57g	**21%**
Protein 15g	

Preheat oven to 400°F. Line a baking sheet with parchment paper.

Slice the eggplant thinly using a mandolin. Rub the eggplant 1½ teaspoons olive oil and transfer to the prepared baking sheet. Bake for 10 minutes or until golden brown and soft.

Add the remaining 1 tablespoon olive oil to a large skillet and heat over medium heat. Add the onion and sauté 3 to 4 minutes. Add the garlic and cook until fragrant, about 1 minute.

Add the mushrooms and cook until they are just tender, about 4 to 5 minutes. Stir in the kale and quinoa, and cook until the kale is wilted slightly, about 2 to 3 minutes. Season with thyme, lemon zest and juice, salt and pepper.

Spoon the filling into the prepared eggplants and roll the eggplant like you do a sandwich or sushi roll.

Serve the eggplant immediately, garnished with parsley and accompanied by the yogurt and additional lemon wedges. Squeeze lemon over them and eat!

DINNER:
Grilled Salmon With Chickpeas
Prep Time: 5m   Cook Time: 20m   Total Time: 25m

7oz salmon fillets
1 tbsp olive oil, divided
½ tsp smoked paprika
1 diced Roma tomato
1oz baby spinach
1 tsp balsamic vinegar
1/2 tsp kosher salt, plus more for seasoning
1/4 tsp freshly ground black pepper, plus more for seasoning
12oz can of chickpeas
1 clove of garlic

Nutrition Facts	
Servings: 1	
Amount per serving	
Calories	**436**
	%Daily Value*
Total Fat 30g	**38%**
Sodium 1297mg	**56%**
Total Carbohydrate 25g	**9%**
Protein 48g	

Season the salmon on both sides with kosher salt and black pepper.

Heat the olive oil in a nonstick pan and fry your salmon filet skin down for 6-7 minutes. Put aside for later.

Meanwhile, drain and rinse 2 cans of chickpeas. Smash the garlic. In the same pan as the one you fried the salmon, add the garlic and sauté until fragrant. Add 1 teaspoon smoked paprika and sauté for 1 minute. Add the chickpeas, diced tomatoes and their juices, 1/2 teaspoon kosher salt, and 1/4 teaspoon black pepper. Stir to combine for 5 minutes.

Add the baby spinach, until just wilted, about 2 minutes. Add the balsamic vinegar. Taste and season with salt and pepper as needed.

Return the salmon, skin-side up, to the pan. Nestle the salmon in the sauce. Continue to simmer for 2 to 5 minutes, depending on the thickness of your fillets. Serve the salmon, skin-side down, with the chickpeas and spinach.

DESSERT:
Carrot Energy Power Balls
Prep Time: 10m   Cook Time: 5m   Total Time: 15m

1 cup pitted dates
½ cup rolled oats
¼ cup chopped pecans
¼ cup chia seeds
1 scoop Optimum Nutrition Vanilla Whey Protein Isolate (or unflavored)
2oz carrots, finely chopped
1 tsp vanilla extract
¾ tsp ground cinnamon
½ tsp ground ginger
¼ tsp ground turmeric
¼ tsp salt
Pinch of ground pepper

Nutrition Facts	
Servings: 22	
Amount per serving	
Calories	45
	%Daily Value*
Total Fat 1g	**2%**
Sodium 329mg	**1%**
Total Carbohydrate 8g	**3%**
Protein 1g	

Pulse dates, oats, pecans and chia seeds in a food processor until well combined.

Add carrots, vanilla, cinnamon, ginger, turmeric, protein powder, salt, and pepper and process until all ingredients are well chopped and a paste begins to form.

Roll the mixture into balls and refrigerate. Enjoy!

Traditional Family Recipes

Fattoush Salad
(Power Romaine Lemon Salad)

Prep Time: 20m Cook Time: 20m Total Time: 40m

1 head romaine lettuce, chopped into bite-sized pieces
1 English cucumber, bite sized slices
1 small red onion, peeled and thinly sliced
1 cup diced tomatoes
1 cup loosely-packed chopped fresh mint leaves
4 radishes, thinly sliced
2 to 3 cups baked pita chips, homemade
1 tbsp sumac

LEMON DRESSING
1/3 cup extra-virgin olive oil
1/4 cup freshly-squeezed lemon juice
1 large clove garlic, pressed or minced
1 tspn sea salt
1 tspn ground sumac

Nutrition Facts	
Servings: 4	
Amount per serving	
Calories	**154**
	%Daily Value*
Total Fat 5g	**6%**
Sodium 339mg	**15%**
Total Carbohydrate 25g	**9%**
Protein 5g	

For the dressing, whisk all ingredients together in a little bowl (or shake together in an artisan container) for 30 seconds. Set aside.

For the salad: Combine the romaine, cucumber, red onion, tomatoes, radishes, mint, and half of the pita chips in a large mixing bowl. Drizzle evenly with the lemon dressing, then toss until evenly combined.

Serve: Serve immediately, garnished with the remaining pita chips, plus an extra sprinkle of sumac and freshly-ground black pepper.

Lentil Soup

Prep Time: 5m   Cook Time: 30m   Total Time: 35m

1 cup red split lentils
5 cups of cold water
1 onion roughly chopped
1 carrot roughly chopped
1 potato roughly chopped
Small pinch of turmeric
1/2 tbsp salt approx.

Wash the lentils in a fine sifter by running them under cool water.
Add the lentils to a pot with the cold-water boil on medium high heat.

Chop the carrot, onion, potato and add them to the lentils along with the turmeric and salt.
Cook for another 20 minutes until the potato is done. Turn off the heat and blitz with a hand blender. Taste and adjust the salt.
Serve in a bowl with a squeeze of lemon and a drizzle of extra virgin olive oil.

Nutrition Facts	
Servings: 4	
Amount per serving	
Calories	**221**
	%Daily Value*
Total Fat 0.6g	**1%**
Sodium 317mg	**14%**
Total Carbohydrate 41g	**15%**
Protein 14g	

Shakshuka
(Spicy Poached Egg Breakfast)

Prep Time: 10m Cook Time: 25m Total Time: 35m.

1 cup of tomato sauce and 3 cups cold water
1 diced roma tomato
1 diced yellow onion
1 clove crushed garlic
50g chopped cilantro
6 eggs

Spice Mix:
1 teaspoon of each cumin, garlic powder, black pepper, turmeric, paprika or chili powder

Heat oil in a pan. Add the diced onion and tomato and cook for about 5 minutes. Add sauce, water, garlic, cilantro, and spice mix. Cook for an additional 1-2 minutes.
Add the eggs. Cover and simmer until the egg whites are cooked, but yolks are still runny.
Remove from the stove top and season with salt and pepper. Sprinkle crumbles of feta cheese, chopped cilantro, and serve with pita bread.

Nutrition Facts	
Servings: 2	
Amount per serving	
Calories	391
	%Daily Value*
Total Fat 31g	**40%**
Sodium 677mg	**29%**
Total Carbohydrate 11g	**4%**
Protein 20g	

Tabouleh
(Green Power Salad)
Prep Time: 10m   Cook Time: 5m   Total Time: 15m

100g bulgur wheat (or cooked quinoa to increase protein)
2 large firm, vine-ripened tomatoes (about 200g) with lots of flavor (roma works well)
1 large bunch (about 100g) fresh flatleaf parsley
20g fresh mint
6 spring onions (scallions), trimmed and very thinly sliced
3 tbsp fresh squeezed lemon juice
2 tbsp extra-virgin olive oil

Nutrition Facts	
Servings: 3	
Amount per serving	
Calories	**234**
	%Daily Value*
Total Fat 10g	**13%**
Sodium 37mg	**2%**
Total Carbohydrate 33g	**12%**
Protein 7g	

Wash the bulgur in cold water couple of times, it would be better if you can marinate it with hot water so it puffs a bit (no more than 10 minutes).
Sieve the bulgur well and transfer to a large dry mixing bowl.
Finely dice the tomatoes, mix them into the bulgur and set aside for a few minutes.
Just before serving, finely slice the parsley and mint as thin as you can.
Add the parsley, mint, spring onions, lemon juice, olive oil and sea salt into the salad and serve directly.
For a twist, add a splash of balsamic vinegar at the end.

Hummus

Prep Time: 10m   Cook Time: 1m   Total Time: 11m

2 15 oz cans of chickpeas drained and washed
1/4 cup tahini
1/3 cup lemon juice
1 tsp salt
1/2 tsp lemon salt
2-3 cloves garlic minced
3 ice cubes
1 tbsp olive oil for topping

Wash and drain the chickpeas very well. Place the chickpeas into a blender with the tahini, lemon salt, garlic, ice cubes, and lemon juice.
Blend them for at least a minute to obtain smooth texture.
Transfer hummus to a plate and spread around. Top with some olive oil and paprika for garnish. Some also like to top with cumin powder.

Nutrition Facts	
Servings: 6	
Amount per serving	
Calories	**600**
	%Daily Value*
Total Fat 16g	**21%**
Sodium 437mg	**19%**
Total Carbohydrate 89g	**32%**
Protein 29g	

Turkey Chili

Prep Time: 10m   Cook Time: 45m   Total Time: 55m

2 tsp olive oil
1 yellow onion, chopped
3 garlic cloves, minced
1 medium red bell pepper, chopped
1 pound extra lean ground turkey
4 tbsp chili powder
1 tbsp ground cumin and smoked paprika
1 tsp dried oregano
¼ tsp cayenne pepper
½ tsp salt, plus more to taste
1 (28-ounce) can diced tomatoes or crushed tomatoes
1 ¼ cups low sodium chicken broth
2 (15 oz) cans dark red kidney beans, rinsed and drained
1 (15 oz) can sweet corn, rinsed and drained

Nutrition Facts	
Servings: 6	
Amount per serving	
Calories	**506**
	%Daily Value*
Total Fat 18g	**23%**
Cholesterol 79mg	**26%**
Sodium 570mg	**25%**
Total Carbohydrate 17g	**62%**
Protein 69g	

For topping: low-fat shredded cheese, avocado, baked tortilla chips, cilantro, low fat sour cream (or Fage 0% Greek yogurt)

Sauté onion, garlic, and red pepper in olive oil for 5-7 minutes, stirring frequently.
Add ground turkey and stir well to break up the meat. Cook until brown. Next add chili powder, cumin, paprika, oregano, cayenne pepper and salt. Mix well.
Add in tomatoes, chicken broth, kidney beans and corn. Bring to a boil, then reduce heat and simmer for 30-45 minutes. Taste and adjust seasonings and salt as necessary.

Molokhia (Green Anti-Oxidant Chicken Soup)

Prep Time: 1h   Cook Time: 1h   Total Time: 2h

300g dry Molokhia (Jew's Mallow)
50g olive oil
17 garlic cloves
2 bunches cilantro, chopped finely
2 tsp salt
1 tbsp dried coriander
Juice of 2 lemons

Chicken Broth:
2 whole chicken breasts	2 bay leaves
5 garlic cloves	½ onion
2 tsp. alt	1 tsp. black pepper
1 tb. olive oil	

Nutrition Facts	
Servings: 4	
Amount per serving	
Calories	**469**
	%Daily Value*
Total Fat 33g	**42%**
Sodium 416mg	**62%**
Total Carbohydrate 70g	**26%**
Protein 8g	

Molokhia is called Jew's Mallow in English. Every country has a different way of making Molokhia. You can find frozen Jew's Mallow is almost any supermarket (if not, check Middle Eastern markets).

We will start by making the broth. Season the chicken breast with salt and pepper. In a deep stockpot add 1 tbsp of olive oil. Then add the chicken and sear on both sides. Add half a gallon of water, bay leaves, cloves, and peeled onion to the pot and bring it to a boil. When the chicken is cooked, set it aside and shred with two forks. Save the broth for later.

For the Molokhia leaves, spread them on a flat surface, pick off any stems and wilted, yellow leaves and discard. Boil water in a large stockpot. Submerge the Molokhia leaves until totally soaked and soft. Place the leaves in a sieve and allow to drain. Usually this takes around 15 rinses.

Peel the garlic and cut in half. Reserve 5 whole cloves of garlic for later. Mash the garlic in a mortar and pestle until nearly liquified.

In a large stockpot, heat the olive oil and add the cilantro and garlic and sauté them until golden. Add the rinsed and squeezed Molokhia leaves and whole cloves of garlic to the mix and sauté for about 5 minutes. Add the sieved broth and bring to a boil. Cook over medium heat for 20 minutes.

Add the shredded chicken breast and lemon juice to the pot. Salt to taste. Let simmer for 5 more minutes. Serve with steamed white rice.

Shish Tawouk (Chicken Kabobs)

Prep Time: 15m Cook Time: 2h Total Time: 2h 15m

¾ cup Fage 0% Greek yogurt
1 tbsp tomato paste
3 tbsp olive oil
2 tbsp lemon juice
3 cloves garlic
1 tsp salt
¼ tsp ground black pepper
1 tsp paprika
1 tsp ground cumin
½ tsp dried oregano
2 pounds (900g) chicken breasts boneless and skinless, cut into 1-inch pieces

Nutrition Facts	
Servings: 8	
Amount per serving	
Calories	279
	%Daily Value*
Total Fat 14g	**18%**
Sodium 400mg	**17%**
Total Carbohydrate 2g	**1%**
Protein 35g	

Mix the yogurt, tomato paste, lemon juice, garlic, olive oil, cumin, paprika, oregano, salt and pepper until well combined.

Place the chicken in the marinade. Mix until chicken is well coated. Cover with plastic wrap and marinate for at least 2 hours and up to 24 hours in the fridge.

Skewer the chicken onto skewers (about 4-5 pieces per skewer).

Grill on an outdoor grill or a grill pan for about 4-6 minutes per side.

Lahem Bi Ajeen Fatayer (Meat Pies)

Prep Time: 35m   Cook Time: 14m   Total Time: 50m

Dough:
½ tbsp sugar
1 tbsp yeast
¼ cup olive oil
1 dash of salt
2 cups warm water (105-110 F)
5 cups all-purpose flour

Meat Filling:
1 ½ pounds ground turkey
1 large onion diced
1 large tomato diced
1 tbsp salt
2 tbsp Arabic 7 Spice (allspice, black pepper, cinnamon, cloves, coriander, cumin, nutmeg)
1 tbsp pomegranate molasses (optional, but very yummy!)

Nutrition Facts	
Servings: 6	
Amount per serving	
Calories	**718**
	%Daily Value*
Total Fat 22g	**28%**
Sodium 1291mg	**56%**
Total Carbohydrate 87g	**32%**
Protein 43g	

Add the sugar, yeast and warm water to a bowl. Rest for 10 minutes. Then add the flour and knead well. Sprinkle some extra water if it's too tough. Slowly add in the olive oil and knead until dough has formed. Let dough rest for half an hour.

Preheat oven to 500 F. Line a large baking sheet with parchment paper.

In a bowl mix the meat filling ingredients.

Roll out the dough into 2.5 inch diameter circles. Add 2-3 tablespoons of the meat mix and press down to cover most of the round pie.

Bake for about 14 minutes until lightly golden brown. Garnish with minced parsley, squeeze of lemon, and crushed red pepper flakes.

Mujadarah
(Syrian Lentil Rice)

Prep Time: 5m   Cook Time: 35m   Total Time: 40m

1 cup green lentils
½ cup white rice
2 onions (1 diced and 1 sliced)
2 tbsp olive oil
4 cups water
1½ tsp ground cumin
1 tsp salt
½ tsp black pepper

Nutrition Facts	
Servings: 4	
Amount per serving	
Calories	347
	%Daily Value*
Total Fat 8g	**11%**
Sodium 593mg	**26%**
Total Carbohydrate 54g	**20%**
Protein 1g	

Boil the lentils in water for 10 minutes on medium heat.

While the lentils are cooking, sauté the diced onion in a small pan with 1 tablespoon of olive oil. Add the cumin and sauté for 1 more minute, set aside.

Sauté the sliced onion in the same pan with a tablespoon of olive oil on medium-low heat until deep golden brown and caramelized. Stir often to prevent the onions from burning. These will be used for garnishing.

Wash the rice thoroughly and add to the lentils along with the sautéed diced onion.

Season with salt and pepper and lower the heat all the way down to low. Cook covered for 10-15 minutes until all the water has been absorbed.

Garnish the Mujadarah with the caramelized onions and serve at room temperature with pita bread and a side salad.

Hashweh Rice
Aromatic Spiced Rice with
Ground Turkey
Prep Time: 15m   Cook Time: 45m   Total Time: 1h

1 pound ground turkey
1 tbsp olive oil
2 cups Jasmine rice, rinsed
4 tbsp olive oil
1 tsp Arabic 7 Spice (allspice, black pepper, cinnamon, cloves, coriander, cumin, nutmeg)
2 tsp Kosher salt (start with 1 tsp if using table salt)
1 tsp black pepper
4 1/2 cups warmed chicken stock or broth
1/2 cup pine nuts
1/2 cup raw almonds, slivered
2 tbsp olive oil

Nutrition Facts	
Servings: 8	
Amount per serving	
Calories	**493**
	%Daily Value*
Total Fat 27g	**34%**
Sodium 1284mg	**56%**
Total Carbohydrate 40g	**15%**
Protein 24g	

Begin by prepping your rice. In a large bowl, cover rice completely with water. Gently rub rice granules in water. Drain water and repeat until water runs clear. It should take about 5-6 rinses.

Heat a heavy-bottomed non-stick pot on medium-high heat, add 2 tbsp olive oil and ground turkey. Brown the meat and break apart using a wooden spoon for about 5 minutes.

Add your rinsed and drained rice to the ground turkey along with 4 tablespoons olive oil and spices (7 spice, salt, and pepper). Stir to combine and lower heat.

Continue stirring your mixture on low for 25-30 minutes until you see all the rice granules separated from one another.

Meanwhile, heat your broth and set aside.

Next, add your heated broth to the rice and meat mixture. Place lid on pot and continue to cook on low heat for 20 minutes.

While your rice is cooking, in a small pan, add your remaining 2 tablespoons of olive oil and pine nuts. Begin toasting on medium heat until just golden brown. Remove and add almonds, repeat same process until golden brown.

Plate your "Hashweh Rice". Top with toasted nuts and fresh chopped parsley. Serve immediately.

Dr. Alo's Famous "Hot as Heck" Grilled Chicken

Prep Time: 10m   Chill Time: 1h Total Time: 1h 10m

1 whole chicken

Marinade:
1 bottle (500ml) low sodium soy sauce
12 oz orange marmalade
100g ginger root
1-2 pcs habanero peppers (more to add more heat)
5-6 cloves of garlic
1 tbsp liquid smoke
1 tbsp citric acid (or the juice of 1 lemon)

Nutrition Facts	
Servings: 4	
Amount per serving	
Calories	**330**
	%Daily Value*
Total Fat 18g	**1%**
Sodium 2950mg	**333%**
Total Carbohydrate 72g	**26%**
Protein 40g	

Mix all marinade ingredients together in a blender. Coat the chicken with a 1/3 of the marinade and save the rest for basting and a dipping sauce later.

Poke the skin of the chicken with a knife so the marinade can seep inside. Marinate for 1 hour. You can also rub some under the skin.

Get your grill grates up to about 400-500 degrees. Place the chicken on the grill. Sear both sides, then drop the temp down to 250 or 300 degrees. Close the lid. Let it slow cook. Watch out for fires. (Thinner pieces will cook quickly like wings while thicker parts like breasts will take longer).
Towards the end, baste the chicken again with the marinade. You can simmer the remaining marinade to thicken it up and make a nice BBQ dipping sauce.

High in sodium, so be mindful if you make this!

Thank you!

I hope you enjoyed this book and these recipes! Please share with your friends and send them the links to buy and download. I have tried to make this book as easy to follow as possible to encourage people to eat healthier and lose weight!

If you want more great recipes and updates, don't forget to go to the website and sign up for the newsletter so you can keep getting updates!

https://DrAlo.net/free